UNSEEN SCIENCE

What Is Motion?

Laura L. Sullivan

Cavendish Square

New York

Published in 2016 by Cavendish Square Publishing, LLC
243 5th Avenue, Suite 136, New York, NY 10016

First Edition

Website: cavendishsq.com

This publication represents the opinions and views of the author based on his or her personal experience, knowledge, and research. The information in this book serves as a general guide only. The author and publisher have used their best efforts in preparing this book and disclaim liability rising directly or indirectly from the use and application of this book.

CPSIA Compliance Information: Batch #CW16CSQ

All websites were available and accurate when this book was sent to press.

Library of Congress Cataloging-in-Publication Data

Sullivan, Laura L. (Laura Lee), author.
What is motion? / Laura L. Sullivan.
pages cm – (Unseen science)
ISBN 978-1-5026-0915-1 (hardcover) ISBN 978-1-5026-0914-4 (paperback) ISBN 978-1-5026-0916-8 (ebook)
1. Motion–Juvenile literature. I. Title. II. Series: Unseen science.
QC133.5.S85 2016
531'.11–dc23

2015022178

Editorial Director: David McNamara
Editor: Andrew Coddington
Copy Editor: Rebecca Rohan
Art Director: Jeffrey Talbot
Designer: Joseph Macri/Amy Greenan
Senior Production Manager: Jennifer Ryder-Talbot
Production Editor: Renni Johnson
Photo Research: J8 Media

The photographs in this book are used by permission and through the courtesy of: Zhu Difeng/Shutterstock.com, cover; Dorling Kindersley/Getty Images, 5; Hal Horwitz/Getty Images, 6; Skip ODonnell/Getty Images, 7; Andrew Rich/Getty Images, 8; Yenwen Lu/Getty Images, 8; Courtesy of the United States Government/GPS.gov, 10; Sgt. Maj. Michael Pintagro/DVIDS, 13; Clockwise from top left: Lynn Seeden/Getty Images, Ruslana Iurchenko/Shutterstock.com, Andrew Lambert Photography/Science Source, 15; Deyan Georgiev/Shutterstock.com, 16; Timothy Clary/AFP/Getty Images, 18; Stockbyte/Thinkstock, 19; Lena Pan/Shutterstock.com, 21; I3alda/Shutterstock.com, 22; Mark Wilson/Getty Images, 23; Corbac40/Shutterstock.com, 24; Steve Hathaway/Getty Images, 25.

Printed in the United States of America

CONTENTS

CHAPTER 1

Understanding Motion

You probably already have an idea what **motion** is. You know when you are moving, and when you are at rest. But even when you don't think you are moving, you really are. Your heart keeps beating; your blood keeps flowing. At an even smaller level, your cells are in motion. Even individual molecules and **atoms**—the things that make up everything in the universe—move.

On a much bigger scale, the Earth **orbits** the Sun, and the Sun moves within the galaxy. Even galaxies move within the universe. Everything in the universe is always in motion. It's just not always the kind of motion we can easily observe.

What Is Motion?

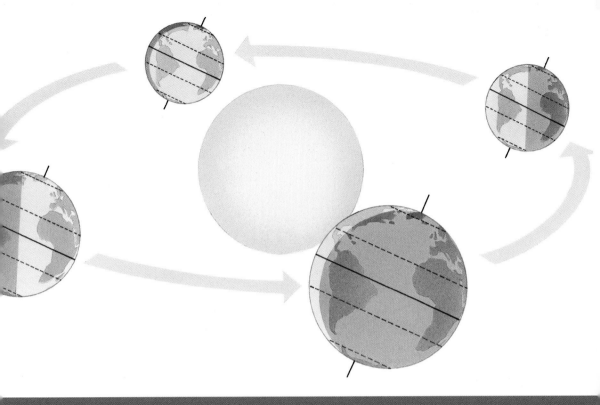

The universe is in constant motion. Even when you are at rest, the Earth is traveling around the Sun.

Newton's Laws

The English scientist Isaac Newton (1642–1727) came up with three laws, or rules, of motion. They hold true for most situations in **physics**. (His laws don't always apply to what is sometimes called "modern physics." This involves objects moving at or near the speed of light, at extreme **temperatures**, inside atoms, and other things scientists are still working to completely understand.)

According to Newton's first law of motion, an object at rest will stay at rest unless some force acts on it. This boulder might stay at rest for centuries until a force acts on it.

The First Law of Motion

Newton's first law of motion says that an object in motion tends to stay in motion, and an object at rest tends to stay at rest. In other words, an object will generally keep doing what it is doing until a **force** acts on it. Another word for that is **inertia**. Examples of force include **gravity**, **friction**, or collision with another object.

A soccer ball sitting in a field is at rest. It will stay that way until some force acts on it. If you kick the soccer ball, you are supplying the force. Then the ball will begin moving. If it was in space, it might

An object in motion will stay in motion unless another force acts on it.

An object with a small mass doesn't need very much force to make it move.

An object with a large mass needs more force to make it move.

move forever. But on Earth, gravity is the force that brings the ball back to the ground. Then the ball might roll for a while. Eventually, the friction of the grass will slow the ball down and stop it. Friction is the force that interferes with the ball's motion.

The Second Law of Motion

Newton's second law states that an object will **accelerate**—or move more quickly over time—when a force acts on it. That acceleration depends on how much force is used, and what the **mass** of the object is. The greater the mass, the more force required to move it. You can make a Ping-Pong ball roll with a tap of your finger. A bowling ball, however, needs a strong push to get rolling.

The Third Law of Motion

Newton's third law says that for every action, there is an equal and opposite reaction. When a force is applied in one direction, there is an equal force in the opposite direction. When a rocket launches, the downward push of the engine is matched by the upward **thrust** of the rocket. The forces are **balanced**.

What Is Motion?

This Chapter Has Shown

Everything is in motion, though we can't always see things moving. Isaac Newton's three laws are true for most kinds of motion. His first law states that an object in motion will stay in motion until a force acts on it. His second law says that an object's acceleration depends on its mass, and how much force is applied to it. His third law says that for every action, there is an equal and opposite reaction.

CHAPTER 2

Experiment with Newton's First Law of Motion

Newton's laws of motion can be seen in action all around you. This **experiment** can help you see some of the ideas more clearly.

Objective

This experiment will allow you to observe the effect of friction on motion. You will see Newton's first law of motion in action.

First, set up the ramp using household objects.

Materials

- A toy vehicle with wheels
- A **ramp** (made from wood, cardboard, or a large book)
- Several (other) books
- A ruler or tape measure
- Paper and pencil

Procedure

1. Build your ramp using a large piece of cardboard, wood, or a book. Prop your ramp up to make an angle. You can use a stack of books to hold the ramp up. This is a mobile experiment. You will have to move your ramp to different locations, so make sure you can keep it at exactly the same angle each time. Measure the height of the ramp to be sure.

2. Hold the toy car with its back wheels at the top of the ramp. Let it go. (Don't push it!) Observe how far it travels across the first **surface** you chose. Measure how far the car traveled from the bottom of the ramp. Write down a description of the surface, and the distance the car traveled.

3. Move the ramp to another location with a different kind of surface. Repeat the experiment and record your results.

4. Find as many different kinds of floors as you can to experiment with. You might try surfaces like vinyl, tile, and carpet. Outside, you can perform the experiment on concrete, slate, or grass. You can also add things to the surface, such as water or baby powder. (Be careful not

Next, let the toy car roll down the ramp and see how far it travels before coming to a stop.

Try the experiment on a variety of surfaces— wood, concrete, dirt, etc.

Measure the distance the car travels on each surface.

Some surfaces have greater friction and slow the car down quickly.

What Is Motion?

to slip! Check with an adult before using water or baby powder indoors.) If you live in a cold climate, you might even be able to make an icy surface by spraying water outdoors.

Questions

- On which surfaces did the car travel the farthest?
- On which surfaces did the car not travel very far at all?
- Why did the car travel farther on some surfaces than on others?
- Think about walking, running, skating, biking, and other activities. Does the type of surface play a part in how fast you can go?

Conclusion

Newton's first law says that once an object is in motion, it will keep moving until something stops it. Friction is one of the things that can slow down or stop moving objects. Friction is the resistance that something feels as it moves over another object.

When you did your experiment, you found that the car traveled farther on some surfaces than on others. On smoother surfaces such as marble, tile, wood, or vinyl, the car traveled for a

Ice has very little friction, so objects sliding on ice tend to stay in motion. This makes icy roads dangerous for pedestrians and drivers alike.

What Is Motion?

You can feel the effect of friction when you coast your bike down a smooth road or a rough grassy hill. You go faster and farther down the smooth road.

greater distance. Those surfaces do not offer as much friction. The wheels of the toy car can move freely on the smooth surfaces.

Other surfaces, though, did not allow the car to travel as far. Rough floors such as concrete slowed the car down. On some surfaces, like carpet or dirt, the car probably didn't travel very far at all. Those surfaces offer much more friction. They exert a force on the wheels, slowing down the car's motion.

CHAPTER 3

Motion in Action

Our bodies use the laws of motion **instinctively**, moving quickly or slowly depending on mass and force. But we have invented even more ways to put the laws of motion to work for us.

We often use the motion of vehicles to do work for us. Many aspects of the science of motion can be seen in an automobile. Inside a car engine, **fuel** (gasoline) is ignited. The explosion of the fuel in a closed space creates expanding gas. It has a lot of **energy**.

That energy is turned into motion. It makes the car's tires turn. The tires push backward against the road. According to

A car engine converts energy into motion.

Newton's third law, this makes an equal and opposite force, pushing the car forward.

Tires and Friction

The car's tires have to strike a perfect balance of friction. If there is too much, then the car wouldn't move well. If there is too little, then it would slide out of control. The tires flatten as the car moves.

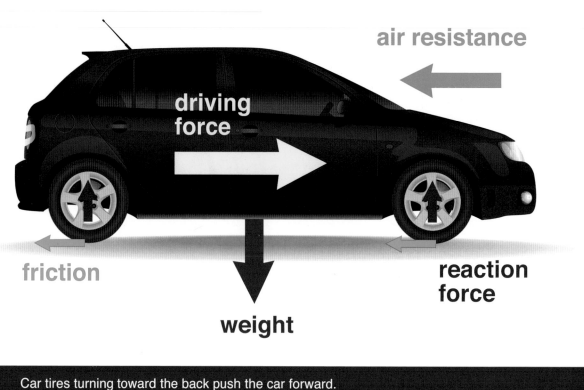

air resistance

driving force

friction

weight

reaction force

Car tires turning toward the back push the car forward.

That puts more of the rubber directly in contact with the rough pavement, helping the tires grip the road and move the car forward. If the tires or the road were perfectly smooth, the tires would slide, and the car couldn't achieve controlled motion.

The grooves in a car's tires help maintain friction when it rains. The little channels give the water somewhere to flow, so the rubber can stay in contact with the road. That keeps the car in steady forward motion, so it doesn't **hydroplane**.

Safety in Motion

Some physicists joke that speed never hurt anyone—it's the sudden stop at the end that's the problem. A car doesn't just have to be capable of motion. It also has to be able to stop. Brakes create friction on part of the wheel. Friction is a force that interferes with motion. Friction slows down the turning of the tires and the car stops.

If a layer of water prevents contact between the tire and the road, friction is reduced and the car can hydroplane.

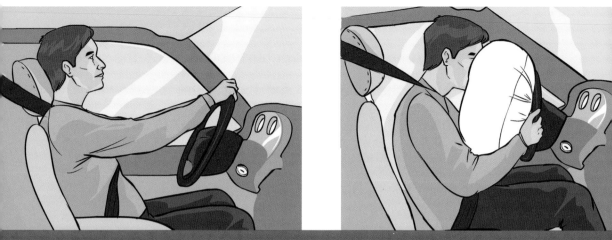

A seat belt makes sure passengers follow the movements of the car, which keeps them securely in place during an accident.

When you ride in a car, you experience Newton's first law of motion. Your body moves at the same speed as the car. But what if the car stops suddenly? If a car hits a tree, it experiences an equal and opposite force, and stops going forward. But what happens to the passengers?

If they are strapped securely in the car with seat belts, they will be part of the car's motion and stop, too. But if they are not belted in, the first law of motion will apply. They will keep going forward even after the car stops. They might even crash forward through the windshield. **Airbags**, which are designed to inflate during crashes, can help stop a person's forward motion.

Car designers consider the laws of motion to help keep drivers and passengers safe in their cars.

This Chapter Has Shown

The laws of motion are at work every time you are in a car. The energy made by the engine is turned into motion. The tires are specially designed to push backward against the road to push the car forward in an equal and opposite force. Safety devices help protect from Newton's first law, so that in a crash you don't fly forward.

Scientists conduct tests to make sure a person is properly restrained in case a car suddenly stops.

GLOSSARY

accelerate To begin to move at a quicker speed.

airbag A cushion in a vehicle that quickly inflates during a crash to help protect passengers.

atom The smallest particle of an element, which cannot be divided.

balance Even or equal distribution of weight or some other factor.

energy The ability to do work; energy can be in many forms including heat, light, electricity, or kinetic (movement).

experiment A scientific process done to test an idea or prove a fact.

force Something that causes a change in motion of an object, such as gravity or air resistance.

friction The force of resistance that happens when one object moves against another.

fuel A substance that provides energy, power, or heat.

gravity The attraction between all objects with mass; on Earth, the force that causes things to fall toward the center of the Earth.

hydroplane To uncontrollably slide on a wet surface.

inertia A tendency to stay in a current state of motion (or rest) unless acted upon by another force.

instinctively Acting without thought or deliberate intention.

mass A measurement of how much matter is in objects; weight can change depending on gravity, but mass does not change.

motion The action of changing position.

orbit The curved path of one body as it moves around another body in space, such as the movement of the Earth around the sun, or the moon around the Earth.

physics The branch of science that studies matter and energy.

ramp An inclined plane or slope between two elevations.

surface The upper layer or outer part of something.

temperature The relative degree of heat as measured by a particular scale, such as Fahrenheit or Celsius.

thrust A force exerted on an object that causes it to accelerate in the opposite direction.

Books

Angliss, Sarah, and Maggie Hewson. *Hands-On Science: Forces and Motion*. New York: Kingfisher Books, 2013.

Lawrence, Ellen. *Motion*. New York: Bearport Publishing, 2013.

Weakland, Mark. *Zombies and Forces and Motion*. North Mankato, MN: Capstone Press, 2012.

Websites

Physics Central

www.physicscentral.com

With physics information for all ages and interest levels, this site also has an Ask-a-Physicist section.

FIND OUT MORE

Physics4Kids

www.physics4kids.com

This site covers many aspects of physics in an easy-to-understand way.

Science Kids: Physics

www.sciencekids.co.nz/physics.html

This New Zealand–based site has pages on all aspects of science, including physics experiments to try at home.

INDEX

Laura L. Sullivan is the author of more than thirty fiction and nonfiction books for children, including the fantasies *Under the Green Hill* and *Guardian of the Green Hill*. She has written many books for Cavendish Square, including two others in the Unseen Science series: *What Is Heat?* and *What Is Gravity?*